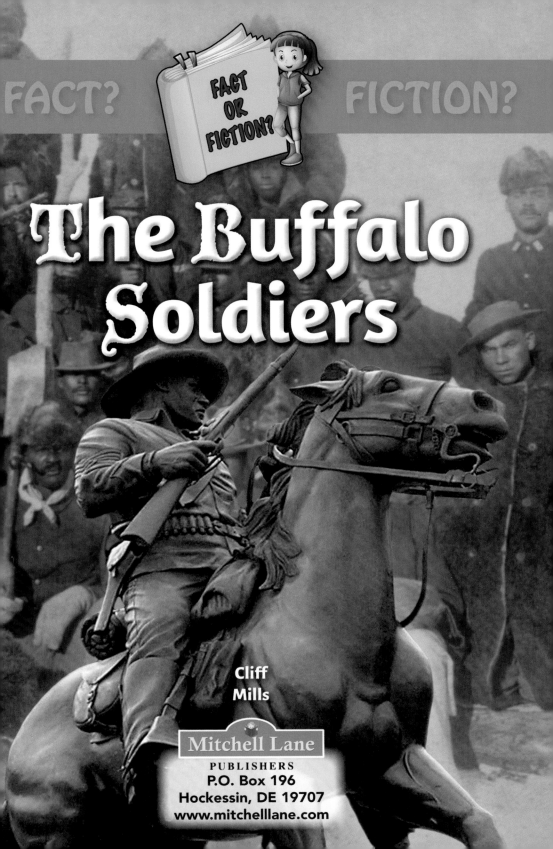

FACT? FICTION?

FACT OR FICTION?

The Buffalo Soldiers

Cliff Mills

Mitchell Lane
PUBLISHERS
P.O. Box 196
Hockessin, DE 19707
www.mitchelllane.com

Mitchell Lane

PUBLISHERS

Printing   1   2   3   4   5   6   7   8

Audie Murphy
Buffalo Bill Cody
The Buffalo Soldiers
Eliot Ness

Francis Marion
Robin Hood
The Tuskegee Airmen
Wyatt Earp

Library of Congress Cataloging-in-Publication Data
Mills, Cliff, 1947–
 The buffalo soldiers / by Cliff Mills.
    pages cm. — (Fact or fiction?)
 Includes bibliographical references and index.
 Audience: Grades 3-6.
 ISBN 978-1-61228-970-0 (library bound)
 1. United States. Army—African American troops—History—Juvenile literature.
 2. African American soldiers—History—Juvenile literature. I. Title.
 E185.63.M53 2015
 355.0089'96073—dc23
                                                                    2015003179

eBook ISBN: 978-1-61228-971-7

                                                                    PBP

CONTENTS

Words in **bold** throughout can be found in the Glossary.

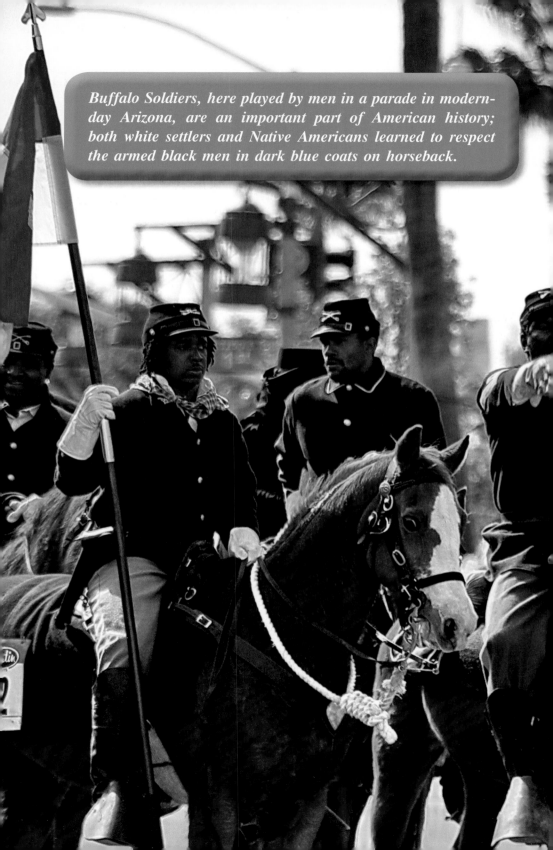

Buffalo Soldiers, here played by men in a parade in modern-day Arizona, are an important part of American history; both white settlers and Native Americans learned to respect the armed black men in dark blue coats on horseback.

CHAPTER 1

The Deadliest Enemy

Sergeant George Jordan and two dozen soldiers from the 9th Cavalry **regiment** of the US Army were exhausted after riding all day. It was May 1880 and they were in western New Mexico Territory, scouting for hostile Indians and protecting a wagon train carrying supplies. It was a harsh land where rattlesnakes and scorpions were not the biggest concerns.

The soldiers stopped for the night. Suddenly a rider appeared with an urgent message. Settlers near Old Fort Tularosa were in danger. The feared **Apache** war chief Victorio and a band of 100 warriors were closing in on them.

Sergeant Jordan knew his horses were worn out and couldn't go anywhere. He asked his men if they were ready to help. He wrote later, "They all said they would go as far as they could."[1]

They marched all night and arrived at the remote settlement at daybreak. Victorio and his band were not there yet. Jordan wrote that when the settlers realized that help had arrived, "They came out of their houses waving towels and handkerchiefs for joy."[2]

Jordan was a 14-year veteran of the **Indian Wars**. He knew what his men had to do. They quickly repaired part of the abandoned fort, and built a new stockade (a high fence). They worked at a furious pace, knowing that they and the fort were all that stood between the settlers and certain death.

At dusk, bullets suddenly began kicking up dirt and desert sand. The settlers rushed into the repaired fort just as Victorio and his warriors attacked. Wave after wave of Indians tried to get into the fort. But the soldiers, aided by their Springfield rifles, Colt .45 revolvers, training, and raw courage, fought them off.

Victorio knew what he was up against. He had often fought these soldiers. The Indians called them "Buffalo Soldiers." They were African-American troops who had proven their skill and bravery in the Indian Wars. Victorio retreated after many of his men died. The settlers were saved.

Historian T.J. Stiles writes that the Buffalo Soldiers had once again "out-marched [and] outfought . . . a foe often considered to be the hardest-marching, hardest fighting, most skillful enemy in frontier history."[3] In fiction, Geronimo was the deadliest Apache war chief. In fact, Victorio was. Both were **guerrilla warriors** who hit their foes and then disappeared, seeming to be everywhere and nowhere. They represented a formidable challenge to the Buffalo Soldiers.

Historians agree that Indians began calling the black soldiers "Buffalo Soldiers" sometime around 1870.[4] The soldiers earned that name after several battles along the Saline River in Kansas. They often charged directly at the Indians, even when they were outnumbered by ten to one.[5] A black soldier in a dark blue uniform on a dark horse may have looked like a buffalo from a distance.[6] Also, their dark curly hair must have reminded the Indians of the hair on a buffalo's forehead.

Historians disagree on whether the term was an insult or praise. William Leckie and many others think it was a term of praise, since the buffalo were so important to the Indians. But other experts, such as Frank Schubert and Ron Field, argue that "Buffalo Soldier" may have been an insult at first, and possibly only later a sign of respect.[7]

The first Buffalo Soldiers themselves almost certainly did not use the term. Only one soldier, Reuben Waller, uses it in writing, and not until 1929.[8] But future generations of black soldiers would proudly use the term and even put it on regiment badges.

At first, most Buffalo Soldiers were freed slaves. In the immediate aftermath of the Civil War, they were organized into four regiments: the 9th and 10th Cavalry, and 24th and 25th Infantry. They were paid $13 a month, not only far more money than they could have earned as civilians but also the same as white soldiers. That was a rare form of equality in a country still divided after the Civil War. The first Buffalo Soldiers reported to **Fort Leavenworth**, Kansas, in 1867, with jobs giving them respect and power. The next generation of Buffalo Soldiers had never been slaves, but still knew **bigotry** and racism. Both generations were tough and determined men who went from being raw recruits falling off horses and wasting water and ammunition to some of the most disciplined and brave fighters the US Army has ever known.[9]

A Buffalo Soldier had his horse, his gun, and his bedroll, and little else, as he rode into a harsh and wild frontier.

CHAPTER 2

Making War and Peace

Major George Forsyth was dying. He had been shot through both legs. He and 50 white **frontier scouts** had been searching for Indians on the plains of eastern Colorado, in September 1868. **Cheyenne** warriors found him and his men first. Forsyth's group was trapped on a small island in the middle of a dry riverbed. They dug holes into the dirt and sand with their hands and knives to protect themselves from Indian bullets and arrows coming from all sides.

The two forces battled each other for eight days. Several scouts were killed, picked off by Indian snipers. Many Indians died from the deadly shots of the frontier marksmen, who were armed with the latest models of rifles and pistols. But the surviving scouts were starving and dying of thirst. Luckily for them, two scouts had somehow escaped early in the battle and made their way to Fort Wallace, in western Kansas.

That was home to several companies of the 10th Cavalry. Company H rode west as fast as possible over the dry grass of the **Great Plains**. They saved the frontiersmen, who gladly took the food and water given them by the black men. The fight would go into Western legend as the Battle of Beecher's Island.

One Buffalo Soldier who was there, Reuben Waller, wrote much later that 2,000 Cheyenne took part in the fight. That added to the legend. But historian Frank Schubert notes that soldiers are usually too busy to make accurate enemy counts in battle.[1] And for the Cheyenne it was not a legendary battle. Schubert adds, "It was a hard fight, but one of everyday happenings of the time."[2]

Old Fort Tularosa and Beecher's Island were two of the approximately 130 battles that an estimated total of 5,000 Buffalo Soldiers fought against Indians in Kansas, **Indian Territory**, Texas, New Mexico Territory, Arizona Territory, and the Dakotas from 1867 to 1891.[3] These battles were fought primarily because the US government made and enforced laws that placed Indians on **reservations**. That policy forced Indians to try to become farmers because they could no longer hunt buffalo. The buffalo had been their source of food, clothing, and shelter. Some Indians made the radical change in **culture** and diet, but many did not. When they left their reservations in search of food and freedom, the Buffalo Soldiers were ordered to return them to the reservations or kill them, depending on who was giving the orders.[4]

The country was divided on whether forcibly placing Indians on reservations was a good policy. Some thought it was "a miserable failure."[5] The Buffalo Soldiers didn't make the policy, but their job was to carry it out.

One of the main reservations in Indian Territory was for the **Kiowa** and **Comanche** tribes. The Buffalo Soldiers needed a fort there. So they built **Fort Sill** in an area with rich grass for horses, clear water from Medicine Bluff Creek, and forests for wood. They cut logs and carved rock out of a quarry. It was backbreaking work.[6] All the time, they were being watched by the Kiowa and Comanche on the reservation.

An *Army & Navy Journal* reporter wrote about the songs the Buffalo Soldiers would sing there at night before Taps (notes from a bugle signaling the end of the day) during the building of the fort. After Taps, "all is still except the howling of the wolf or the bark of the coyote, relieved by the 'tum, tum, tum' of the rawhide drum in the Indian camp."[7]

The Fort Sill site was carefully chosen for its grassland and forests, making it one of the longest-lasting forts in the West.

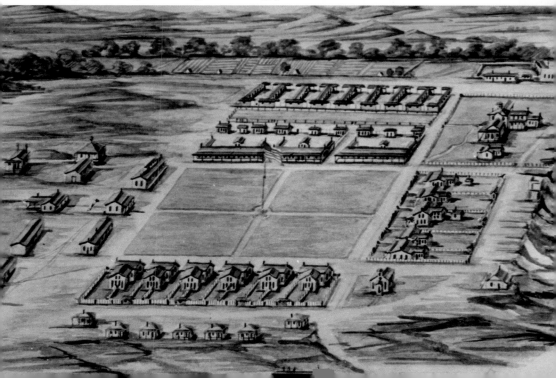

Buffalo Soldiers served as armed guards for many stagecoaches and their passengers, protecting lives and valuables.

CHAPTER 3

The Guardians and Explorers of the West

General William T. Sherman had been a Civil War leader known for his brutal but effective tactics. He became one of the main commanders of the US Army in the West after the war, enforcing the policy of putting Indians on reservations. He was not sympathetic to the Indians. When told that a certain Comanche chief was "a good Indian," Sherman replied, "The only good Indians I ever saw were dead."[1] Sherman also believed that killing all the buffalo was "the only way to bring lasting peace and allow civilization to advance" because it would force the Indians to stay on reservations.[2] When he came to Indian Territory in 1871 to investigate Kiowa and Comanche raids on wagon trains in Texas, the Buffalo Soldiers became his bodyguards.

Sherman called for a meeting at Fort Sill with its commander Colonel Benjamin Grierson and several Indian chiefs. They gathered at Grierson's headquarters. Several Buffalo Soldiers were on guard.

Sherman demanded to know who was raiding the wagon trains. Satanta, one of the Kiowa chiefs, said his people were starving on the reservations because the government agents were not keeping promises of food made in treaties. He said his people must raid to live. Sherman became angry. He said Satanta was under arrest.

A bad situation got worse quickly. Satanta and other chiefs had guns. Hundreds of Kiowas were nearby. Word of the arrest spread to them. The only force that could keep the peace was the Buffalo Soldiers. Historian William Leckie writes, "A moment's loss of nerve or an instant 'trigger-itch' could have launched a bloodbath."[3]

The Buffalo Soldiers kept their cool, even with guns aimed at them and their officers. There was no bloodbath that day because of their discipline and restraint. Satanta and other chiefs surrendered. They knew that they did not have enough firepower, ammunition, and reinforcements.[4]

The Buffalo Soldiers also had another important task at about the same time: exploring. Beginning in the summer of 1871, all four regiments took part in explorations of the **Staked Plains**. These were tens of thousands of square miles of unmapped territory in northwest Texas and eastern New Mexico Territory. Early Spanish explorers got so lost in the treeless region that they marked trails with stakes made of the bones and skulls of buffaloes.

The Buffalo Soldiers were given the dangerous job of mapping the territory, noting water holes and any areas that could be used for ranches and farms. One expedition left **Fort Concho** in Texas in July 1875. More than two hundred Buffalo Soldiers and wagons drawn by six-mule teams headed west. Soon, the desert began to take its toll. One historian writes that the men "suffered desperately from heat, dust, and thirst. The exhausted bluecoats [Buffalo Soldiers] were tied in their saddles."[5] They were only saved when they reached the Pecos River. They kept going, having to choose between being safe and staying close to water, or risking death and mapping more. They chose to risk death and map more.

But the explorers were destroyers as well. They burned any abandoned Indian lodges and villages they found. Some had been abandoned very quickly, just before they got there. They helped destroy a culture as well.

Two years later, the Staked Plains would kill four Buffalo Soldiers. The water holes mapped on the earlier expedition had dried up. Many of the soldier-explorers were new recruits, and didn't conserve water. After days without it, one officer wrote that the "men [were] gasping in death around us."[6] Some survived by following an old Indian trail to a small lake shimmering in the moonlight. The officer wrote, "such hurrahs and firing of guns you never heard in your life."[7]

Because of the explorations and mapping, a land boom began. That was good news for white settlers and bad news for the remaining Indians roaming the land who had been able to hide in the Staked Plains. More waves of white men followed: miners, cattle rustlers, and thieves. The West got wilder before it got tamed.

Buffalo Soldiers were ready for anything: here they have the tools for building, exploring, and policing.

Being the Law

Lincoln County, in the southern half of New Mexico Territory, had a reputation of having more murderers and thieves than almost any other place in the West in the late 1870s.[1] Gangs fought each other and the federal government over money, gold, silver, land, water, and cattle. The gangs were killers themselves or they hired killers like the legendary William Bonney, also known as Billy the Kid. Bonney had been hired by one of the most violent gangs, the McSweens.

Fiction tells us about Western gunfights in showdowns on dusty main streets. Facts tell us that most murders involved armed men killing unarmed men in cold blood, out of sight.[2] Fiction tells us about brave sheriffs and marshals with true grit tracking down the bad guys. Facts tell us about town sheriffs who were often afraid to arrest criminals. Even if they did, juries were often too afraid to convict.[3]

The town of Lincoln was a center of this lawlessness. One hot July day in 1878, a Buffalo Soldier from nearby **Fort Stanton** rode into town. He was shot at by the McSween gang. Soon afterward, Buffalo Soldiers and white infantrymen from the fort came into town with a **Gatling gun** and a brass cannon. They set up camp in the middle of the town, aimed the cannon at the McSween headquarters, and said that if another soldier was fired on, the cannon would answer.[4] The local sheriff took courage from the soldiers, and set fire to the headquarters. Several men were shot down as they fled the flames, though Bonney escaped. People learned that the Buffalo Soldiers would defend their own in a measured way, as soldiers. They didn't shoot up the town.

The Buffalo Soldiers had to become the law in many places. For example, some land in the Indian Territory had not been assigned to any tribe. Railroad executives, land dealers, farmers, and ranchers all wanted a piece of the action. The land was federal property. But that didn't stop a group called the **Boomers**, named after the land boom they expected.

Starting in the spring of 1879, the Boomers made nine separate attempts to set up illegal settlements in Indian Territory.[5] Buffalo Soldiers from **Fort Riley**, Kansas, and other forts had to enforce the law and throw them out. Sometimes these were forceful confrontations, when the Buffalo Soldiers from the 10th Cavalry had to tie up the would-be white settlers, throw them back into their wagons, and return them to Kansas. But often the soldiers peacefully and quietly asserted federal law. They even shared their bacon and beans with the same people they had to round up.[6] They brought justice, but they brought mercy as well.

Congress later opened that land, and more. In 1890, white settlers could move into parts of the **Lakota** reservations in northwestern Nebraska and southeastern Dakota Territory. The fear and betrayal felt by the Lakota helped spread the **Ghost Dance** religion among them. Ghost Dancers promised that the land would be soon be covered with new soil that would bury white people. The new white settlers were terrified. Chief Sitting Bull was thought to be a leader of the Ghost Dancers, and he was killed while being arrested. That brought a last cycle of war.

The 7th Cavalry slaughtered at least 150 Indian men, women, and children in the valley of Wounded Knee Creek on December 29, 1890. The next day the same troops were trapped near the Pine Ridge reservation by hundreds of Indians wanting revenge. The 9th Cavalry rode 100 miles in one day and came charging across the snow to rescue the white soldiers.[7] The Buffalo Soldiers were protectors, but this time they protected those on the wrong side of history.

That was the last major operation by the Buffalo Soldiers in the West. The many jobs they performed had a lasting effect. The technology that the Buffalo Soldiers helped bring had changed the West. They had strung thousands of miles of telegraph lines and protected many railroad construction crews. As result, many Western towns grew.

With the growth came more fences and the closing of the **open range**. Some Buffalo Soldiers left the Army and became cowboys on ranches.

Spanish troops in forts and bunkers fought hard as they fired at point-blank range, but the Buffalo Soldiers and other American troops won the day in Cuba in 1898.

CHAPTER 5

The Bravest Men Anywhere

Fiction has the Buffalo Soldiers story ending at the close of the Indian Wars in the early 1890s. But facts write one more chapter. The soldiers had to fight yet another famous battle.

America went to war against Spain in 1898. At that time Spain owned Cuba, and Americans were upset by how Spain treated Cuban rebels who wanted independence. All four Buffalo Soldier regiments took part in an invasion of Cuba in June to free it from Spanish control.

The key to capturing Cuba was capturing Santiago de Cuba, the island's second-largest city. And the key to capturing Santiago de Cuba was a series of hills called San Juan Heights. Spanish forces were dug into those hills, with forts, trenches, and plenty of cannons.

When the Buffalo Soldiers and other American troops got to the hills, the Spanish were waiting for them. The Americans were shot at mercilessly as they tried to advance uphill. They returned fire with a vengeance. An Army report said the Buffalo Soldiers "poured lead into every door, porthole, and rifle pit in sight."[1]

On July 1, the 10th Cavalry found itself fighting next to the 1st US Volunteer Cavalry, known as the Rough Riders because some were cowboys. Their second-in-command was Theodore Roosevelt, who would soon be president of the United States. The two cavalries, on foot, worked their way up Kettle Hill, part of San Juan Heights. The fighting was vicious. Many officers were shot and sergeants had to assume leadership. When a soldier carrying the American flag was shot, another would pick it up.[2]

At one point, the Rough Riders were pinned down. They couldn't advance. The 10th charged up and helped save them.

Twenty-six Buffalo Soldiers died that day, one of the worst days in their history. Many more were wounded. A sergeant in the 10th Cavalry later wrote, "The dead and wounded soldiers! It was indescribable . . . . I truly hope I may never see it again."[3] Frank Knox, a Rough Rider, wrote about the Buffalo Soldiers, "I never saw braver men anywhere."[4]

Most newspaper accounts of the battle didn't mention the Buffalo Soldiers. The men were asked to stay in the background when pictures were taken. But the US Army knew what had happened. Four Medals of Honor—the country's highest military decoration— were awarded to members of the 10th Cavalry as a result of their actions in Cuba.[5]

The Buffalo Soldiers had to pass through Georgia and Florida on their way to Cuba. They had often been insulted and harassed by whites in the West. The worst were settlers in Confederate uniforms.

"Seeing black men in uniform sometimes inflamed whites to riot and lynch,"[6] writes historian Henry Louis Gates, Jr.

They felt even more hatred in the South. As always, some Buffalo Soldiers ignored the racism, and some reacted. "Even when responding to civilian insults and outrage, they remained soldiers,"[7] notes Frank Schubert.

Their years in the West had made many of them demand respect. The *Tampa Morning Tribune* wrote that the men of the 25th Infantry "insist upon being treated as white men are treated."[8] On their way home from Cuba, they were treated as heroes in a parade in Long Island, New York, but could not eat in most restaurants in Kansas City.

All four Buffalo Soldier regiments fought in Cuba, one of the few times they were all together.

The alert Buffalo Soldier shown in this monument at Fort Leavenworth, Kansas, is well-armed and ready to react to any crisis.

During the twentieth century, they continued to serve honorably in the Philippines, along the Mexican border, and during World War I and World War II. Finally US armed forces became fully integrated and units composed entirely of African Americans were disbanded.

In recent years there has been a revival of interest in the Buffalo Soldiers. On July 25, 1992, 20,000 people came to Fort Leavenworth, Kansas (the first fort the Buffalo Soldiers were assigned to) for a Buffalo Soldier ceremony and the unveiling of a statue. The statue shows a Buffalo Soldier on his horse, a rifle in his hands, and a pistol at his side. The chairman of the **Joint Chiefs of Staff**, Army General Colin Powell, said, "The powerful purpose of this monument is to motivate us. To motivate us to keep struggling until all Americans . . . have every chance to achieve their dream."[9]

The courage and iron will of the Buffalo Soldiers continue to inspire to this day. But their story is not simple. For some people the Buffalo Soldiers were at least partly villains. They helped destroy Indian culture, even if they were just carrying out orders. For others, they stood up against racism and explored vast territories, so are heroes. Still others focus on their bravery as soldiers. From any viewpoint, their history is a vital part of America's history.

FACT OR FICTION?

FICTION: The Buffalo Soldiers were only Indian fighters.

FACT: They were also explorers, builders, law enforcers, and guards.

WHY IT MATTERS: Their role in changing the American West in the last decades of the 1800s was important. As law enforcers and guards, they most often did their work peacefully and quietly. Violent acts get more coverage in history, but peaceful enforcement should be noted as well. As explorers, their courage was shown over and over. They went to places others would not go.

FICTION: The Buffalo Soldiers fought Indians in large battles with hundreds of men on each side.

FACT: Most battles were small.

WHY IT MATTERS: History is often made by a series of small conflicts, not a few large ones.

FICTION: Buffalo Soldiers captured Billy the Kid.

FACT: They didn't.

WHY IT MATTERS: Their role as law enforcers was important, and doesn't need to be added to with misinformation.

FICTION: The Buffalo Soldiers could not defend themselves against racism and bigotry.

FACT: They found ways to defend themselves.

WHY IT MATTERS: Their responses to racism were effective and measured. They didn't shoot up towns, but people knew they would react if they were attacked.

FICTION: Sheriffs and marshals always enforced the law in the West.

FACT: Sometimes they didn't. They were too afraid of revenge, and knew juries were often too afraid to convict.

WHY IT MATTERS: The role of the Buffalo Soldiers as law enforcers was important. Local law enforcement often needed help.

FICTION: The Buffalo Soldiers are forgotten.

FACT: In the past 25 years, they have been given significant recognition. The statue at Fort Leavenworth was only a start. Unmarked graves of many Buffalo Soldiers now have markers.

WHY IT MATTERS: We need to study and remember history. That means studying and remembering the people who made it.

FICTION: The Buffalo Soldiers were purely heroic.

FACT: Their story is not just pure heroism. They were often in terrible situations and ordered to help destroy cultures.

WHY IT MATTERS: It is important to have a balanced knowledge of historical events.

Chapter 1: The Deadliest Enemy

1. T.J. Stiles, "Buffalo Soldiers." *Smithsonian Magazine*, December 1, 1998, p. 90.
2. Ibid.
3. Ibid., p. 94.
4. Ron Field and Alexander Bielakowski, *Buffalo Soldiers: African American Troops in the US Forces 1866–1945* (Oxford, United Kingdom: Osprey Publishing, 2008), p. 36.
5. Ibid.
6. John W. Ravage, *Black Pioneers: Images of the Black Experience on the North American Frontier* (Salt Lake City, UT: University of Utah Press, 1997), p. 43.
7. Frank N. Schubert, *Voices of the Buffalo Soldier: Reports and Recollections of Military Life and Service in the West* (Albuquerque, NM: University of New Mexico Press, 2003), p. 47.
8. Ibid.
9. Field, p. 47.

Chapter 2: Making War and Peace

1. Frank N. Schubert, *Voices of the Buffalo Soldier: Reports and Recollections of Military Life and Service in the West* (Albuquerque, NM: University of New Mexico Press, 2003), p. 23.
2. Ibid.
3. Ron Field and Alexander Bielakowski, *Buffalo Soldiers: African American Troops in the US Forces 1866–1945* (Oxford, United Kingdom: Osprey Publishing, 2008), p. 22.
4. Schubert, p. 52.
5. Michael Bellesiles, *1877: America's Year of Living Violently* (New York: The New Press, 2010), p. 68.
6. William H. Leckie and Shirley A. Leckie, *The Buffalo Soldiers: A Narrative of the Black Cavalry of the West*. Revised edition (Norman, OK: University of Oklahoma Press, 2003), p. 48.
7. Field, p. 40.

Chapter 3: The Guardians and Explorers of the West

1. Clinton Cox, T*he Forgotten Heroes: The Story of the Buffalo Soldiers* (New York: Scholastic, 1993), p. 47.
2. Ibid., p. 69.
3. William H. Leckie and Shirley Leckie, *The Buffalo Soldiers: A Narrative of the Black Cavalry of the West*. Revised edition (Norman, OK: University of Oklahoma Press, 2003), p. 62.
4. Michael Bellesiles, *1877: America's Year of Living Violently* (New York: The New Press, 2010), p. 79.

5. Paul H. Carlson, "William R. Shafter, Black Troops, and the Opening of the Llano Estacado, 1870–1875," *Buffalo Soldiers in the West: A Black Soldiers Anthology*, Eds. Bruce A. Glasrud and Michael N. Searles (College Station, TX: Texas A&M University Press, 2007), p. 63.
6. Cox, p. 94.
7. Ibid.

Chapter 4: Being the Law
1. Ron Field and Alexander Bielakowski, *Buffalo Soldiers: African American Troops in the US Forces 1866–1945* (Oxford, United Kingdom: Osprey Publishing, 2009), p. 61.
2. Michael Bellesiles, *1877: America's Year of Living Violently* (New York: The New Press, 2010), p. 63.
3. Frank N. Schubert, *Voices of the Buffalo Soldier: Reports and Recollections of Military Life and Service in the West* (Albuquerque, NM: University of New Mexico Press, 2003), p. 78.
4. Field, p. 62.
5. William H. Leckie and Shirley Leckie, *The Buffalo Soldiers: A Narrative of the Black Cavalry of the West*. Revised edition (Norman, OK: University of Oklahoma Press, 2003), p. 254.
6. Ibid., p. 255.
7. Field, p. 81.

Chapter 5: The Bravest Men Anywhere
1. Ron Field and Alexander Bielakowski, *Buffalo Soldiers: African American Troops in the US Forces 1866–1945* (Oxford, United Kingdom: Osprey Publishing, 2008), p. 101.
2. Ibid., p. 106.
3. Ibid., p. 108.
4. Ibid.
5. Henry Louis Gates, Jr., *Life Upon These Shores: Looking at African American History, 1513–2008* (New York: Alfred Knopf, 2011), p. 209.
6. Ibid.
7. Frank N. Schubert, *Voices of the Buffalo Soldier: Reports and Recollections of Military Life and Service in the West* (Albuquerque, NM: University of New Mexico Press, 2003), p. 115.
8. Field, p. 97.
9. Fort Leavenworth Garrison Public Affairs Office. http://garrison.leavenworth.army.mil/

Apache (uh-PATCH-ee)—tribe of Native Americans who used to live and hunt in southwest Texas, New Mexico, southern Colorado, and Mexico, especially known for living and fighting in the mountains

bigotry (BIG-uh-tree)—an attitude that views other people with fear or hatred based on their race, religion, place of birth, or other feature

Boomers (BOO-muhrz)—settlers who tried to claim lands in the Indian Territory after 1879, before it was opened up to settlers ten years later

Cheyenne (shy-ANN)—Native Americans who used to live and hunt on the Great Plains and now have reservations in Montana and Oklahoma

Comanche (co-MAN-chee)—Native Americans who used to live and hunt on the Great Plains, in eastern New Mexico Territory, southeastern Colorado Territory, southwestern Kansas, and western Indian Territory

culture (KULL-chur)—the way of life of a people, including its beliefs and art

Fort Concho (FORT CON-cho)—a fort in west Texas near the city of San Angelo and a headquarters for the 10th Cavalry

Fort Leavenworth (FORT LEV-uhn-worth)—a fort just north of Leavenworth, Kansas and original home to the Buffalo Soldiers

Fort Riley (FORT RY-lee)—a fort in north-central Kansas built in 1853, where both the 9th and 10th Cavalry regiments were stationed at various times

Fort Sill (FORT SILL)—a fort in Lawton, Oklahoma built in 1869, mostly by Buffalo Soldiers

Fort Stanton (FORT STAN-tuhn)—a fort in New Mexico built in 1855 along the Rio Bonito and home to the 9th Cavalry for several years

frontier scouts (fruhn-TEER SCOUTZ)—guides and explorers who knew where to find trails, water holes, and other useful sites in the American West as well as track hostile Native Americans

Gatling gun (GAT-ling gun)—an early rapid-fire gun invented by Richard Gatling used during the Civil War and after

Great Plains (GREAT PLANEZ)—an area that extends from the Mississippi River west to the foothills of the Rocky Mountains

guerrilla warriors (guh-RILL-ah WAR-ee-urs)—fighters who use hit-and-run tactics to attack, fight, and then disappear

Ghost Dance (GOAST DANCE)—a religious movement among Native Americans in late 1800s in the belief that dead and living could unite with their spirits and bring peace and prosperity

Indian Wars (IN-dee-uhn WARZ)—conflicts fought between Native Americans and the US Army in the West after the Civil War, until 1891

Joint Chiefs of Staff (JOYNT CHEEFS uhv STAFF)—senior military officials who represent the US Army, Navy, Air Force, Marine Corps, and National Guard

Kiowa (KY-oh-wuh)—Native Americans who used to live and hunt in the southern Great Plains and now have reservations in Oklahoma

Lakota (la-COH-tah)—Native Americans who are part of the Sioux nation and used to live in and hunt in the Great Plains, especially in Dakota Territory, and now live primarily in five reservations in western South Dakota

open range (OH-puhn RANJ)—unfenced land where cattle roam freely

regiment (REDGE-uh-muhnt)—military unit with 10 or 12 companies, each of which has 80 or more soldiers

reservation (reh-zuhr-VAY-shun)—area of land occupied and managed by a Native American tribe

Staked Plains (STAKED PLANEZ)—an area of roughly 40,000 square miles in eastern New Mexico and northwestern Texas that is part of the Great Plains; formerly called the Great American Desert

Bellesiles, Michael. *1877: America's Year of Living Violently*. New York: The New Press, 2010.

"Buffalo Soldiers." National Park Service. http://www.nps.gov/yose/historyculture/buffalo-soldiers.htm

"Buffalo Soldiers of the American West." Scientific and Cultural Facilities District. http://www.buffalosoldiers-amwest.org/index.htm

Carlson, Paul H. and William R. Shafter. "Black Troops, and the Opening of the Llano Estacado, 1870–1875." *Buffalo Soldiers in the West: A Black Soldiers Anthology*. Eds. Bruce A. Glasrud and Michael N. Searles. College Station, TX: Texas A&M University Press, 2007.

Cox, Clinton. *The Forgotten Heroes: The Story of the Buffalo Soldiers*. New York: Scholastic, 1993.

Dobak, William A. "Fort Riley's Black Soldiers and the Army's Changing Role in the West." *Buffalo Soldiers in the West: A Black Soldiers Anthology*. Eds. Bruce A. Glasrud and Michael N. Searles. College Station, TX: Texas A&M University Press, 2007.

Field, Ron and Alexander Bielakowski. *Buffalo Soldiers: African American Troops in the US Forces 1866-1945*. Oxford, United Kingdom: Osprey Publishing, 2008.

Fort Leavenworth Garrison Public Affairs Office. http://garrison.leavenworth.army.mil/

Gates, Henry Louis, Jr. *Life Upon These Shores: Looking at African American History, 1513–2008*. New York: Alfred Knopf, 2011.

Glasrud, Bruce A. and Michael Searles, eds. *Buffalo Soldiers in the West*. College Station, TX: Texas A&M University Press, 2007.

Lamm, Alan K. "Buffalo Soldier Chaplains of the Old West." *Buffalo Soldiers in the West: A Black Soldiers Anthology*. Eds. Bruce A. Glasrud and Michael N. Searles. College Station, TX: Texas A&M University Press, 2007.

Leckie, William H. and Shirley A. Leckie. *The Buffalo Soldiers: A Narrative of the Black Cavalry of the West*. Revised edition. Norman, OK: University of Oklahoma Press, 2003.

Leiker, James. "Black Soldiers at Ft. Hays, Kansas, 1867–69: A Study in Civilian and Military Violence." *Buffalo Soldiers in the West: A Black Soldiers Anthology*. Eds. Bruce A. Glasrud and Michael N. Searles. College Station, TX: Texas A&M University Press, 2007.

Ravage, John W. *Black Pioneers: Images of the Black Experience on the North American Frontier*. Salt Lake City, UT: University of Utah Press, 1997.

Schubert, Frank N. *Voices of the Buffalo Soldier: Reports and Recollections of Military Life and Service in the West*. Albuquerque, NM: University of New Mexico Press, 2003.

Stiles, T.J. "Buffalo Soldiers." *Smithsonian Magazine*, December 1, 1998.

FURTHER READING

Barnett, Tracy. *The Buffalo Soldiers*. Broomall, PA: Mason Crest, 2002.

Flanagan, Alice. *The Buffalo Soldiers*. North Mankato, MN: Compass Point Books, 2005.

Glaser, Jason. *Buffalo Soldiers and the American West*. North Mankato, MN: Capstone, 2006.

Orr, Tamra. *The Buffalo Soldiers*. Hockessin, DE: Mitchell Lane, 2009.

Stovall, Taressa. *Buffalo Soldiers*. New York: Chelsea House, 1997.

ON THE INTERNET

Buffalo Soldiers: African Americans in the Frontier Army.
http://www.electronicfieldtrip.org/buffalo/teachers/classroom_L04_html

National Park Service: "Buffalo Soldiers."
http://www.nps.gov/yose/historyculture.buffalo-soldiers.htm

US Military: "African Americans in the US Army."
http://www.army.mil/africanamericans/timeline/html

INDEX

ABOUT THE AUTHOR

Clifford Mills is a writer and editor living in Jacksonville, Florida. He has written biographies of many historical and world leaders, including Hannibal, Angela Merkel, Pope Benedict XVI, Lord Baltimore, and Francis Marion. He has also written about many sports and entertainment figures. Two of his grandparents came to live in Indian Territory just before Oklahoma became a state.